WRITE BLOODY PUBLISHING
NASHVILLE, TN

Special thanks to Co-editors Amber Tamblyn & Mindy Nettifee of the Blacksmith Collective.

Foreword © 2008 Derrick Brown
First Edition, Write Bloody, January 2008
For information about purchases contact: writebloody@gmail.com
Manufactured in Tennessee, USA

Book design by DZN CRZ.
Type set in Helvetica and Franklin Gothic.
Edited by Derrick Brown.
Cover image by Robyn Anderson.
Back cover image by M. Wignall.
Proofread by Saadia Byram.

www.writebloody.com

The Last American Valentine

Illustrated poems to seduce and destroy

WRITE BLOODY PUBLISHING

NASHVILLE, TN

"LOVE IS LIKE A ROLL OF TAPE.
IT'S REAL GOOD FOR MAKING TWO THINGS ONE,
BUT JUST LIKE THAT ROLL OF TAPE,
LOVE SOMETIMES BREAKS OFF BEFORE YOU WERE DONE.

ANOTHER WAY THAT LOVE IS SIMILAR TO TAPE,
THAT I'VE NOTICED
IS SOMETIMES IT'S HARD TO SEE THE END.
YOU SEARCH ON THE ROLL
WITH YOUR FINGERNAIL."

-FLIGHT OF THE CONCHORDS

Contents

FOREWORD 9

JEFFREY MCDANIEL ART BY BRANDON LYON & MATTHEW CARVER 11

MINDY NETTIFEE ART BY JENNIFER DAVIS 21

JACK HIRSCHMAN ART BY MATTHEW CARVER 29

BUCKY SINISTER ART BY MATTHEW CARVER 35

CRISTIN O'KEEFE APTOWICZ ART BY BINGHAM 41

ANIS MOJGANI ART BY ANIS MOJGANI 53

MICHAEL CIRELLI ART BY BRANDON LYON 65

JOHN GARDINER ART BY DANNY SIMON 75

BEAU SIA ART BY JENNIFER DAVIS 12

BUDDY WAKEFIELD ART BY BRANDON LYON 81

LYNNE PROCOPE ART BY JENNIFER DAVIS 12

NATHAN WILLETT ART BY DANNY SIMON 12

VICTOR INFANTE ART BY DANNY SIMON 12

AGNETA FALK ART BY WENDY PENG & RICHARD SWIFT 12

RICHARD SWIFT ART BY RICHARD SWIFT 12

RICK LUPERT ART BY JENNIFER DAVIS 12

ROGER BONAIR-AGARD ART BY RICHARD SWIFT 12

AMBER TAMBLYN ART BY ROBBY MOORING 12

SHAPPY SEASHOLTZ ART BY ROBBY MOORING 12

MICHAEL ROBERTS ART BY JENNIFER DAVIS 12

STEPHEN LATTY ART BY BRANDON LYON 12

MICHAEL C. FORD ART BY MATTHEW CARVER 12

MICHAEL MCCLURE ART BY MATTHEW CARVER 12

BRENDAN CONSTANTINE ART BY BINGHAM 12

DERRICK BROWN ART BY MATTHEW CARVER 12

FOREWORD

These are love poems. Yikes!

The traffic, the television, the wrong city, the noise of failure can turn us cynical to the gross sap of blatant affection. This book is a fresh tackle towards love.

Come at this book quiet and ready. Come at this book with un-sarcastic amazement for that melancholy, drifting and striking feeling, whether you have it, want it, need it or wonder about it. This book is a one-of-a kind mash: a mash–up of amazing artists known and unknown with brilliant authors that I am honored to serve.

This book of romantic poems and illustrations was meant for you to read to or give to someone. If you bought it for yourself, give it to someone woo-able when you are done. This project made me notice how drawings or photographs transformed the mood of the news articles I read. It enhanced the mood like music to a film. The poems selected were chosen for spirit or a stab at being brutally sultry. It was intended to be read by all glittering chest throbbers.

This collection will live beyond Valentine's day due to the generous authors and artists who poured such quality toward this project. When I used to think of Valentines day, I'd think of the old American gangland massacre, lonely stress and hollow chocolate. This book is better than a teddy bear holding a heart.

-Derrick Brown

THE POEMS OF JEFFREY MCDANIEL

BY BRANDON LYON

THE QUIET WORLD

In an effort to get people to look
into each other's eyes more,
the government has decided to allot
each person exactly one hundred
and sixty-seven words, per day.

When the phone rings, I put it
to my ear without saying hello.
In the restaurant I point
at chicken noodle soup. I am
adjusting well to the new way.

Late at night, I call my long
distance lover and proudly say
I only used fifty-nine today.
I saved the rest for you.

When she doesn't respond, I know
she's used up all her words
so I slowly whisper I love you,
thirty-two and a third times.
After that, we just sit on the line

and listen to each other breathe.

BY MATTHEW CARVER

ABSENCE

On the scales of desire, your absence weighs more
than someone else's presence, so I say no thanks

to the woman who throws her girdle at my feet,
as I drop a postcard in the mailbox and watch it

throb like a blue heart in the dark. Your eyes
are so green – one of your parents must be

part traffic light. We're both self-centered,
but the world revolves around us at the same speed.

Last night I tossed and turned inside a thundercloud.
This morning my sheets were covered in pollen.

I remember the long division of Saturday's
pomegranate, a thousand nebulae in your hair,

as soldiers marched by, dragging big army bags
filled with water balloons, and we passed a lit match,

back and forth, between our lips, under an oak tree
I had absolutely nothing to do with.

BY MATTHEW CARVER

THE ARCHIPELAGO OF KISSES

We live in a modern society. Husbands and wives don't
grow on trees, like in the old days. So where
does one find love? When you're sixteen it's easy,
like being unleashed with a credit card
in a department store of kisses. There's the first kiss.
The sloppy kiss. The peck.
The sympathy kiss. The backseat smooch. The we
shouldn't be doing this kiss. The but your lips
taste so good kiss. The bury me in an avalanche of tingles kiss.
The I wish you'd quit smoking kiss.
The I accept your apology, but you make me really mad
sometimes kiss. The I know
your tongue like the back of my hand kiss. As you get
older, kisses become scarce. You'll be driving
home and see a damaged kiss on the side of the road,
with its purple thumb out. If you
were younger, you'd pull over, slide open the mouth's
red door just to see how it fits. Oh where
does one find love? If you rub two glances, you get a smile.
Rub two smiles, you get a warm feeling.
Rub two warm feelings and presto-you have a kiss.
Now what? Don't invite the kiss over
and answer the door in your underwear. It'll get suspicious
and stare at your toes. Don't water the kiss with whisky. It'll turn bright
pink and explode into a thousand luscious splinters,
but in the morning it'll be ashamed and sneak out of
your body without saying good-bye,
and you'll remember that kiss forever by all the little cuts it left

on the inside of your mouth. You must
nurture the kiss. Turn out the lights. Notice how it
illuminates the room. Hold it to your chest
and wonder if the sand inside hourglasses comes from a
special beach. Place it on the tongue's pillow,
then look up the first recorded kiss in an encyclopedia: beneath
a Babylonian olive tree in 1200 B.C.
But one kiss levitates above all the others. The
intersection of function and desire. The I do kiss.
The I'll love you through a brick wall kiss.
Even when I'm dead, I'll swim through the Earth,
like a mermaid of the soil, just to be next to your bones.

THE POEMS OF MINDY NETTIFEE

BY JENNIFER DAVIS

HOW TO GET UNDER MY SKIN

first off, you can stop looking for the zippers.
i hid those long ago, when my two sisters
and twelve-year-old boys everywhere
made rather athletic headway exploiting my soft spots,
disguising insults as compliments i wouldn't discover
until later, in therapy,
like bummer cracker jack prizes.

get subtle.
start with how much you love orangesicles.
start with jokes about Egon Schiele and pedophilia.
start with lame stories from summer camp,
your first awkward salty kiss.

nostalgia is anesthesia.
i'm gripped by how soft you remember humiliation—
that summer you were grounded,
how you mapped the route out of that house, that town, that promise.

there's small openings everywhere:
the last time you saw your mother,
how you picture her sleepless nights on your sleepless nights.
how you save your best punch lines.
bust one out for me.
i'll weaken like a nurse in a massage chair.
i won't notice i'm tearing up.

lean in and smell my shampoo.
let it get dark.
i go down when you figure out how close i came,
just by looking me in the eye.
when we compare childish suicide attempts with hot sauce and aspirin.
i go down when you cast shadows on my shadows,
when it doesn't scare you that i don't know how to flinch.
when you ask me for nothing.   23

BY JENNIFER DAVIS

YOUR NEW GIRLFRIEND IS REALLY NICE

you are an impossible birthday party.
you are cloud climbing.
you are muscle relaxant archery.
i was never a straight shooter with you,
so i'm telling you now
while i've got this strange bravery messing my chest:
i love you like Mexican wrestlers love their outfits.
i miss you like graffiti misses clarity.
i want to crack open for you like a sinner on Sunday.
when i see you kiss another woman
my arm hairs form armies of Elliott Smiths
sifting the wind for some soft suicide song.
you're the naughty punctuation mark i've always been looking for.
you're the electric chair that completes my sentence,
the starving wolverine in my mailbag of wholesome thoughts.
i am afraid of regrets. in my dreams they rise up
like froth mouthed horses, apocalypse black and freaking out.
when i'm awake, i can trick myself into believing almost anything.
it's not magic. it's cereal optimism.
but i'm not buying our someday.
your gravity is moonshine.
it's not the real dance of two heavenly bodies,
or even the bumping of two cake forks at the dessert table.
i just wanted to let you know i know. i just wanted to warn you,
i'm signing up for vanishing lessons.
if i ask to you to meet me on a windy pier somewhere
overlooking the sandy blue cash of the Pacific,
if i ask you to wear your best wool coat,

don't show.

ЛЮБИМАЯ

your love is like Russian:
i don't understand it,
but i like the way it sounds.

i know that if i listened long enough,
i could learn to speak it,
and eventually, to mean what i say

THE POEMS OF JACK HIRSCHMAN

BY MATTHEW CARVER

BLUE

Love comes over me
Like someone who walked
Away and left her white dress
With the little blue flowers

Behind. Behind, behind
Going into the future
Radiantly naked. What am I
To do with it? Put it on?

I don't wear dresses. I love
What's inside them. But
This one's so sad and alone
I'll just let it lie

Awhile on my chest,
Against the curve of my arm
And just let blue flowers be
Blue.

BY MATTHEW CARVER

PATH

Go to your broken heart.
If you think you don't have one, get one.
To get one, be sincere.
Learn sincerity of intent by letting
life enter because you're helpless, really,
to do otherwise.
Even as you try escaping, let it take you
and tear you open
like a letter sent
like a sentence inside
you've waited for all your life
though you've committed nothing.
Let it send you up.
Let it break you, heart.
Broken-heartedness is the beginning
of all real reception.
The ear of humility hears beyond the gates.
See the gates opening.
Feel your hands going akimbo on your hips,
your mouth opening like a womb
giving birth to your voice for the first time.
Go singing whirling into the glory
of being ecstatically simple.
Write the poem.

A POEM BY BUCKY SINISTER

1

Where is she? he asked
In the pit, I said.

She bounded out
all sweat & converse

hold my jacket, she said
I'm going back in

Dude, he said
She's crazy about you

2

She wakes in fog
emerges from mist

By noon
she blows sea wind

teases & flirts
with storms till dark

her night
warmer than day

BY MATTHEW CARVER

3

The bike went down
hook slide into gravel pit

She took my helmet off
and pulled my face in her hands

4

With every junkie I buried
The Velvet Underground
sounded sadder than before

But when I saw you dance
to Sweet Jane before breakfast
it never sounded so joyous

THE POEMS OF CRISTIN O'KEEFE APTOWICZ

AFTER READING OLD UNREQUITED LOVE POEMS

If I didn't think it would make me appear crazy still,
I'd apologize to you for having been so crazy then.

Reading the poems I had written about "us"
resurrected all that nervous heat, reminded me

of the insistent stutter of my longing,
how I could never just lay it out there for you.

The answer, clearly, would have been
no, thank you. But perhaps that tough line

would have been enough to salvage
all that was good and woolly about us:

your laugh, the golden ring I'd always
stretch a story for; the pair of mittens

we'd split in the cold so we'd each have
a hand to gesture with; how even now,

the paths we took are filled with starry wonder
and all that bright limitless air. I'm sorry

I could never see myself out
of the twitching fever of my heartache,

that I traded everything we had for
something that never ended up being.

But if I could take anything back, it wouldn't be
the glittering hope I stuck in the amber of your eyes,

or the sweet eager of our conversations.
No, it would be that last stony path

to nothing, when we both gave up without
telling the other. How silence arrived

like a returned valentine on that morning
we finally taught our phones not to ring.

BY BINGHAM

HOW I SPENT MY SUMMER VACATIONS

Eating my own weight in microwave pizza.

Not getting kissed.

Forgetting basic math skills.

Loathing movies featuring girls who go to horse camp, especially if those girls get kissed.

LONG DISTANCE RELATIONSHIP

Hooray!
Look at me! I'm an idiot!
I'm in a long distance relationship!

Yeah! This rocks! I love being
Really really really far away
from him!

Really really really far away
from him all the time!

It's great!
Look at me! On the plane ride home!
I'm on the plane ride home and
I'm crying! This rocks!

I wish I could write more
but I'm crying too hard!
I mean,
I'm ROCKING too hard!

Life rules!

INBREEDING

I am very much against inbreeding.
Except when you say that
you love me like a sister.

BY JENNIFER DAVIS

I AM SMARTER THAN HER

and that is my only consolation.

DOWN THERE

This is how your refer to your genitalia.
This is also where your mother told me,
while standing at the basement door,
I could find some ice cream.

THE POEMS OF ANIS MOJGANI

BY ANIS MOJGANI

CARPENTRY

I want to make you moonbeams out of fallen leaves
I want to make a house to hold your sleep

BY ANIS MOJGANI

THE MANUAL

squeeze 20 grapes in your cheeks
bite down
spit watermelon seeds
i bet you five pieces you can't spit 'em further than me
kick a can
chase trains
wave at strangers
drive an imaginary submarine
make one out of a box
sleep on a floor with a blanket and a flashlight
draw birds
live forever
plant a tree
write your fist on a wall
run for no reason down the middle of the block
laugh at something funny
smile at sweetness
hold your fingers around it so it doesn't fall
find a dark row in a movie theater
and make out with me
your kisses are a game of horseshoes
i wish i were playing beneath the stars
fat and wet with light
high in the full black sky
so big and silent
it can carry us through this crazy thing
dance under it
listen for the sounds the fields make
the tongues the trees are speaking in
the love the leaves are making with the wind
swallow it down
this is church
your teeth tiny doors

BY ANIS MOJGANI

IN THE HAYSTACK I DREAMED OF BEING A DENTIST FOR YOU

I heard a boy in a window one night make a wish on your skin
he wished however far he may be
that he will shoot any and all of the mountain lions that ever come for
you
will leave a coat built from rabbits on your doorstep for when you are
cold
and when you are sick
set a bowl of soup on your sill
tap twice
and sit in the haystacks while you drink it down
stay there whittling a whistle until you are sound asleep
and next to your fucking beauty of a face
set that whistle down softly
for you to kiss should you ever need him to come to you
he is chipping away at a star
trying to work it loose out of the large jaw of the night
to bring it back down to your ears
it sounds like you
it has your softness
one night when the two of you were walking down the street
he heard a boy in a window
make a wish on your skin
mistaking it for something else
no mistakes were made

BY ANIS MOJGANI

THERE'S GRIZZLIES OUT THERE AND THEY'LL HOLD YOU WARM

I hear the chains of a dog behind me when I walk
but nothing's there
I look like a mountain man
and am beginning to feel more and more like I look
like a man
who is a mountain
but wants to be a river

swim in me girl

sit awhile
teach my skin how to skip stones for you
I want you to swim in me

THE KNIFE IS A DANCE

there's a song in my ears and right now it's making me think of you ann
and of the night sky like a broken air conditioner
humming loudly
pulling a breeze
between our legs
with our bicycles
and that summer
how I would wander
behind wheels and dreams
both running on empty
cutting the highways and telephone wires with my lungs and my eyes
hoping I'd stumble into your breasts and your vanilla tree
and how I wanted to inhale whatever it was that you are
and I don't feel that way no more
but damn
your eyes burned a hole through my spine
and I remembered that beautiful women sometimes taste like glass
and sometimes they laugh the same way
but there were red moons to shoot with arrows
and raspberries to steal
and I wanted to empty spray paint cans with my lips that summer
spitting paint like a dolphin
across the back weed train yard electric fences of new orleans
and home?

home,
how you held me like a handshake

a piece of paper
I wrote your bones across mine and learned how to stand up again
we battered ourselves against the buildings
the little boys bellow we battered our bodies upon the daisies! upon
the graves!
the dead danced!
the dead danced!

THE POEMS OF MICHAEL CIRELLI

BY BRANDON LYON

BALLOON

*Michael, you can't expect the world from me, when my feet
are hardly on the ground,* she said. And also, *I want to hollow
you out and make a sleeping bag of you.* And again, something
along the lines of, *I feel like a wild bird, perched on you.* One more
time, he wanted to hear, *hold me baby baby baby*, while they rolled
around the bed like a cement mixer—He didn't know what
to expect: a levitating lover? a confused camper? turkey vulture?
He worked on his helium tricks nightly, under a boxcar constellation,
below a nervous cuckoo. He said, *The world is yours, and I made you
grass slippers.* And also, *I've pitched tent for you, on the campus of my bed.*
And again, something along the lines of, *My heart is a birdfeeder. Home.*
One more time, she wanted to hear, *anything for you anything for you,
easy,* because that's how she liked her cake—So he whipped up
a balloon, from the blank husk of his body. Aimed it at Puerto Rico.
A silk string around his toe. A head full of motley feathers.
If you're gonna be up there, he said, *hold me baby
baby baby.*

SHER-HOLDER

It is the time of year when the trees
look like pumpkins and the pumpkins have
teeth. They are both all lit up. In the park,
they talk about poetry. She explains: *In Pakistan,*
the elders sit around and recite verses to each other.
He aims for a laugh: *In Rhode Island,* he says, *my family*
sits around a table of antipasto playing poker for pennies.
She continues: *When they like the verse, they go 'va*
va va va.' He replies: *In San Francisco, when they like the verse,*
they snap their fingers. On the trail, they crush
twigs under their heels. In bed, they rub their bodies
together like two wires, but instead of making love,
they make fire. The birds high up are like circling silver
dollars. *The verses are called shers,* she said, *pronounced*
shares. He was thinking up a way. *I told my parents*
about you, she said. She loves how he navigates words
like this: gives trees teeth. Last night, after fire-making,
he read her thirty-two Rumi poems. They laid on their backs
and said a prayer. He asked, *I wonder which God will hear this?*
Today he says, *I am your sher-holder.*

BY BRANDON LYON

HONEY

In the dream, she was back
in Pakistan and she called
to tell me about the man she was
leaving me for, whose *Islam*
matched hers, and he was from
Iran and had *long delicate fingers*
like driftwood
chopsticks and he rolled rice
into *grape leaves* and melted *fruits*
down to dark colors and I was so
concerned with lips
and boundaries - trying to slant
the conversation to did they *kiss?* -
as she talked about the *lamb*
he roasted, the *chutneys* he served
her from wooden spoons
and I needed to know how far
it went and she told me how *soft*
the *eggplant* became from fire,
the *couscous perfect* as embryos, she kept
on and on about *dates, honey, plums...*

KISSING TURTLES

There are those who get off
by putting their head into the mouth
of an alligator, or lion. Paiute Indians are initiated
by sneaking up on a grizzly and smacking it
on the ass. In Key West, fishermen try to snatch
barracudas out of the ocean with their bare hands.
There is a man in New Zealand that rides
on the back of ostriches, and a woman
in Calcutta who plucks the venom from cobras
with her fingers. But I've taken to kissing turtles.
First I paint a bright red arrow on her front door.
I turn the switch on my legs to *slowmo.*
I hang a rabbit's foot from my ear for good luck
and rev the purple motor of my tongue
like a juicer. When a turtle comes out for the kissing,
she is soft as bubblegum, smooth as ribbon.
She repeats her one word over and over: welcome
welcome, welcome welcome welcome

EMBRACE

On the day of the Embrace, the subway car
was packed as a pill bottle. Each bend of the tracks
forced touch between the anxious passengers.
The advertisement above the door had an airbrushed
picture of the actor Jerry Orbach, and urged us
to consider eye donation—as he had, postmortem.
Some people were moved, and others spooked by the idea
of those old showbiz eyes stuffed into the skull
of a little Asian girl. The train kept filling like the downside
of an hourglass. It started slowly:
two stranger fists touched on the handrail, then cautiously,
pinky fingers crept over one another—interlocked.
Then, a black hand enveloped a white one.
Next, a Hasid hooked his fingers through the belt loop
of some hip-hop jeans. Finally, Puerto Rican sisters
on their way to Hunter College locked arms with a banker
like monkeys in a barrel. No one was startled, nothing was sexual.
As the momentum shifted more, an elderly woman
took the glasses right off a young man's face, and softly rubbed
her hands all over his nose, lips, ears.
Strangers looked each other in the eyes, deeply.
They held each other like poles as the train rocked along its tracks.

THE POEMS OF JOHN GARDINER

BY DANNY SIMON

BLACK SWAN

If Love comes pulsing like a south swell
in the rain-pelted jungles of my heart,
palm fronds slick as enamel
blood hot as fire,

I will take off my clothing
and bathe in moonlight like a child
awkward and stunned-
layers of loneliness will vanish,
gauze will clear from my eyes
like clouds releasing the sun.

Love has nothing to do with feelings,
it's tangible as a coming storm;
there's one road we're born for
all we need is a footpath-
if I can walk with you,
the ground will be there
even when the road is lost.

DANCING IN THE NIGHT

Of all romantic hideaways for lovers to cuddle and make love, 8th Ave. in NYC is not even on the desperation list, yet there we were for three years, creating our own heat when the pipes froze every February, the chorus girl and the actor, and I will never forget one night when we crossed the great sensual divide, stuck together with bliss, having swallowed each other whole and eaten any morsels that may have remained, sheets wet with cresting foam and steaming vapors as winter nightwaxedfreshandeasedbackintoourroom, bothofusshaking, seamed together like cloth, nerve endings smoldering as if they were embers still glowing in a bonfire just gone out, and she, suddenly laughing. said, "I can die now," and I said the same as we stretched our arms upward palm to palm until I reached past her, and we wound up around each other like string returning from a kite when the wind gives it up, and my arms kept going round and round about her, clasping as if she were a finger for my rings, safe until Spring, amorphous as cocoons, feeding on each other's beating heart; and if our chest cavities had cracked apart, we would have disappeared into each other and fertilized a glorious hybrid seed, a grafted flower sprouting from sprinkled sheets.

THE POEMS OF BEAU SIA

REVERSE ENGINEERING

we may end tomorrow,
like paris' youth.

but i want to believe
you're forever
like affordable drinking water.

i'd ask you to live in the now
with me,
but both of us are tired
of that marketing scam,

and i just want to hold
the parts of you
that can't be sold.

let's share our tragedies
so we don't become textbooks
filled with omissions,

let's give our faults a chance,
knowing
they don't have to be validated
by oprah
to be beautiful.

we've been taught so many saviors.
maybe it's time to save us
from chasing
the playlists of others.

the soundtrack of love is not
a fixed point in the sky.

our wishes should only reflect
the people we wake up as,
and not
the people
the world sees us as.

so here's my lack of eloquence,
and here's my shotty imagery,
and here's my lack of regard for
form
in the face of feelings
i'll label love,

because i don't respect
any authority
that would try to quantify
the ache
you inspire me with.

let's learn each others'
past in an attempt
to reverse engineer love.

before we learned to
not get burned by the stove.

before we saw
institutions crumble all around us
in the name of.

before we felt loss
that would cripple weaker men.

before we came into
all the words spoken
by other people

about
how we should feel

about these hearts

we've
been given.

when the explanation
didn't exist,

and in the moment
before terrors were imposed on us,

we will love.
no punchline.
no fancy statements.
no perfect structures.

we will love.

EXCERPT FROM WINE WATER

i can feel your sigh
through the glass.

in another country,
a bartender misses
how you
put out cigarettes.

the magic your hair casts
in a room full of compromises
and vodka.

i'm learning
it's a tragic video game,
competing with the past.

tiring when i remind you
where you've been burned
by breathing.

i'm aching to hear
the turning of a doorknob.

receive a handwritten invitation.
end this prolonged stay.

BY MATTHEW CARVER

enter the places
only a child has been to.

hold the blanket
that only knows how to comfort.

warm up the bed
until you get here.

THE POEMS OF BUDDY WAKEFIELD

BY BRANDON LYON

PRINT FLOCKING

He wrote to you with firecracker chalk
on a blackboard background

from a free-standing landing pad
held together by choir claps

over buttercups spraying
out the mouths of doves.

Getting to his point
would require starting over

at the outer loop
of your ripple effect

swinging monkey bar style
arm over arm

parallel to parallel
minding the gaps.

Sometimes it takes a deeper breath
to hover on holy

against the current.
back to where the rock dropped.

He wasn't falling out of love with you.
He was falling out of ways to get there.

GNOME CHAMPSKY

Your favorite singer released her only book in a 20-year career.
Your father bought it for you behind your back.
He was determined to get it autographed and send it off to your first
day away at school.

He looked like a denim garden gnome
with varicose veins.
Just in front of the calluses on his ears were three purple clumps of
Honey-I-Shrunk-the-Chow-Mein-Noodles*** slung like wet sand from a
cup across the pudgy peaks where his nose met his cheeks. I coulda
kissed 'im. All those dumb mistakes in his eyes, like he failed to keep
out the slugs for you.

The way I fell in love with your father was in the way he waited there for
over three hours after everyone told him it wouldn't be possible to get
an autograph. The way I fell in love with your father was in the way he
was so in love with you, the way he stuck around even though he knew
he'd fail by your standards.

He asked if I could help make the autograph happen but I don't keep
that kind of influence laying around. If I could have any superpower
in the universe it would be to fix it. I'd be FIX IT MAN. But I couldn't fix
this. I remembered the way you probably curled up in his belly and
asked him for things he couldn't afford, how the kids made fun of your
ugly dress, and the way you resented him for doing his best.

The way I fell in love with your father started at half-past noon by a tour bus in an alley of Boston where it was cold enough that I lost my boys to my hips, my walk to their shift, and my tears to the flaking freeze of your father's desperate breath. He was trying to prove that, despite the gone flowers and his wilted way of getting buried by winter, he stands guard with a water hose in case you still grow up in flames.

*** That's right. I referenced one of America's most historic movies for this poem.
**This poem is based on a true story. The father at least got an actual autographed copy of the book from the tour manager who traded him for his copy.

A POEM BY LYNNE PROCOPE

BY JENNIFER DAVIS

HERE COMES THE SUN

You suspect the rum
for my sudden stubborn
but the truth is
all day you say goldenrod
and marigold. You lean
into a woman you don't know
to say, I like your hair, it is beautiful.
You make friends
and I don't know anyone
over the age of six
who still does that.

I'm told, a good sentence
requires a complete idea.
You defy me at every
small turn of the wrist but
the sun believes in your
house; she wants to
slip in, to study your
air, to follow you
into your quiet places,
indeed, the sun wants most
to mean, to be found bare,
flawed and going to fat,
rounder and rising
in your kitchen. Is this
a complete idea? I ask

because I know you
only need a small turn
to change the way the light
you see sits on the wall,
or slips in thru a glass
on the window-sill to
dapple the ceiling or
open your throat on a sigh.
I ask because you could lie
but you prefer to notice
how particular a shade
of gold is needed to turn
an entire body into fire.

BY JENNIFER DAVIS

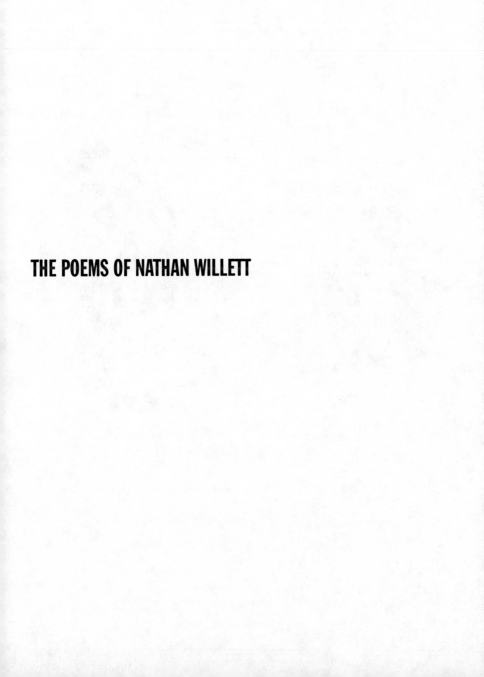

THE POEMS OF NATHAN WILLETT

BY DANNY SIMON

EXPENSIVE TASTES

Strings attached, fake eye lashes
broke apart the piggy bank for petty cash.
Sensitive sister, blushing don't stare
watch the children squabbling in the square.
Tip my hat, low windows
once I saw you naked, there was nothing to show.
Piano plays, sonata tempo.
Of all the girls of in our class, she's the most refined.
I'd like to be there in the morning
when you wake up.
May be pipe dreams, but come Easter
we could pack up.
I'd like to show up, at your door step
wearing a windsor tie my neighbor tied.
And meet your family, compliment cooking
drink the beer that your uncles are brewing.
Flat out refuse, to take that job.
Just because I'm poor don't mean I can't be a snob.
Strawberry hair, fair freckled skin
waiting like a creep outside cotillion.
Shy expression, shawl on her shoulders
bought this house with money that your grandfather stole.
Much too young, save imagination,
ruin an elegant girls reputation.
And when they ask me my occupation:
I'm a-prayin' and working on my patience.

I got no good friends in politic parties.
Her aunt's taking away my car keys.
Mass lets out, rolling smokes for trades,
drink my weight in coffee at the penny arcade.
Rows of shoes, shelves of jewelry:
Momma's dyeing her hair in the vanity.
Daddy's watch too tight,
try silver spoon for size,
harder than a needle through a camel's eye.
Folks gather 'round the table find their place,
boy, if that girl don't have expensive tastes.

MAGLITE

You knew me well enough to snoop in my bedroom when I wasn't home.
Under my rug you spotted
Coffin black scuttling bugs, collected.
In my dresser... a molotov cocktail,
under my pillow... a police maglite.

I walked in and smiled a large 'whoops.'
You could've called me a loose cannon.
I would've sat there and sobbed,
You could've called me a pervert and I would've lost my job,
You could've called me a scaredy cat and I'd be lost
and scratching at another's leg.

Cheap shots aside, You moved into me
like milk pours, like the projects,
and said "I'm renovating you. For good."

BY DANNY SIMON

THE POEMS OF VICTOR INFANTE

WHEN I SAY "I LOVE YOU" I MEAN ...

You echo static // girl on the steps, in the crowd.
      the undiscovered frequency // smile an incantation.
Call this love. Call it chain lightning, juggled hand-to-hand //
      and *Nothing up my sleeve* // and *Don't touch that dial.*
And *Believe:*

What reduces me to end-of-the-radio-band gibberish;
what pulses still, when all my magic tricks, revealed.

ARETHA IN STATIC (RADIO EDIT)

1.)
Just past where the Mass Pike hits
The New York Thruway,
Aretha breaks through
100 bands of static,
a voice to absolve the dead.

Bubblegum pop and dog-tired
classic rock dissolve
in notes, fresh and vital
as when "Chain of Fools"
was new,

insistent as thoughts
of the redhead typing
back home, the voice
that tugged me away
from California,

melted a nation between us:

a song in the static,
suddenly, undeniably
clear.

2.)
No name for the tesseract space between us: airport terminal affection,
billowing steam in the right hand of Shiva. Communication breakdown.
The swallowing of sky.

Radio band crackle: Nothing real. Everything.

3.)
Postcards from England. E-mail from the Bay. We wave across airports,
pass on freeways.
We've Survived abandoned theaters and empty bookshops.
Bottles crashed against cliff faces, broken glass slid into the ocean.

I love you for that.

Our distance is cell phone reception and dial-up modems.

4.)
There are no diminishing returns.
The heart holds all these, and more.

BY DANNY SIMON

ALEXANDRIA

Unspeakable
ghost knowledge
tapping at the
back of my teeth.
I hold flames to
my lips, try to
burn this from
me, but it just
rises again as
steam, settles as
condensation,
soaks again into
my skin.

I wanted to tell
you a desert, but
my throat was
Sirocco, words
simmering in arid
dust,
evaporating. The
sandstorm of this
flakes at my skin,
longs to kiss the
earthquake of
you, until I am
swallowed com-
pletely, until I am
gone.

UNFINISHED BUSINESS (RADIO EDIT)

1.)

It's a bad habit, leaving things behind:
my favorite Zippo on a nightstand in Cairo,
the earring gift vanished in the California surf,
a language-barrier shattering kiss in Holland,

they linger like unresolved chords, burn in half-lives,
diminished over time, cast into relief by a love
that flares like daylight.

Sometimes I find my way back,
trails looping to familiar terrain.
Sometimes they turn up on their own,
unexpected and thunderclap sudden.

2.)

Love poses unanswerable questions:

What is the proper disposition of the salad fork?
Does this existential angst make me look fat?

Red wine by the glass, or by the bottle?
Is the weight of this conversation worth the inevitable earthquake?

Did I leave my credit card on the checkered tablecloth,
my wallet in the backseat of the Nissan Sentra I sold in 1990?

3.)

I am typing as the sun rises, head full of songs.
I don't know all the lyrics.

I was always the one who drifted, enraptured
by moving trains, with a wind-chilled hitchhiker's thumb,
re-reading the radioactive thesaurus of love
for some rephrasing, some new way to speak,
breath transforming to smoke,

earthquakes that twist railroad tracks,
underscore garages and coffee shops,
a distant rumbling shaking the knickknacks,
rattling the ink off pages and table settings,

these things return to me,
aftershocks I must acknowledge
as my own.

PLAY ONE MORE FOR MY RADIO SWEETHEART

10.) I knew about snapped bass strings and the boy in Long Beach, knew you'd stripped yourself of even your name, but I wasn't alarmed until I'd heard she'd rescued your cats.

9.) It's always been split lips and sheathed knives between us, but you were there when the bitch threw rocks at her windows, when the boogeyman slammed fists against her door at 3 a.m., and for that, I'm grateful.

8.) Your wedding photos chill me – I search the crowd shots to find my own face lost amid the smiling friends in ill-fitting tuxedoes, like some specter of me was there to dance with you.

7.) You laid the guitar in the closet and it disappeared entirely, but sometimes you can hear familiar chords echoing through the house's rafters, each song a funeral dirge.

6.) The radio bears no songs of you and me and what we've lost to the needle; when the world condenses to the back seat of a station wagon, no food for days, the body propelled by small snakes slithering in your veins. No more.

5.) No exorcism for ghosts that walk like the living, that telephone desperate and starving from gas station parking lots, begging change for reheated burritos, building a mausoleum of Styrofoam wrappers.

4.) The boy's no good for you, will chip away at you until you are something less, a bauble to be placed on a shelf.

3.) She is gone, and her absence rattles like the wind through an empty garage, the whistle of air kissing emptied glass bottles. It haunts you at night when your eyes snap open, disturbed from sleep by a song your fingers still recall how to play.

2.) I miss hearing you sing.

1.) I should have been there.

VIEW FROM THE SANDCASTLE'S TURRET

These silica walls were never meant to be home,
but still I find myself by starlight,
hands deep in earth, tide soaking shredded clothes,

sculpting battlements of sand and eucalyptus bark,
seawater mortar, brine-drenched air drowning
the taste of this from my mouth, and still
I scratch absently at the barriers, particles
wedging beneath fingernails.

Memory: Palm at the small of her skinny back;
Fingers gently tracing the brittle bone of her,
as she curled like a question into my lap,
bit my lip, kissed the blood away,
folded herself into the shadows, gone.

Memory: Reclined on a second-hand couch,
not touching, mouthful of ocean, moonlight
caressing your face, not touching, spark of us
burns at the back of our necks, not

unfathomed whispers in the dark,
distant sea shanties; Unjoyous ocean
burbling through flooded foundations,
the collapse of elaborate towers
that were never meant to last.

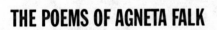

THE POEMS OF AGNETA FALK

BY RICHARD SWIFT

OCTOBER

You come dancing through the bush-wood,
the door opens to the shade of my skin,
your tongue at the corner of my mouth,
my openings widening
as I kneel in the wind of your breath.

My skin smoothes to a plain of desire
behind closed eye-lids
centuries destined to flood
swirl to a long, sharp light,

the hallelujah chorus
of mismatch and match,
the network of lanes
trickling into one pool
of flesh, one nation.

Can you see me?
I'm here naked and safe.
Yet there is a shift.
It's not love. It's love.
A slow burning fire
lit on a damp October evening
long before my birth, before you.

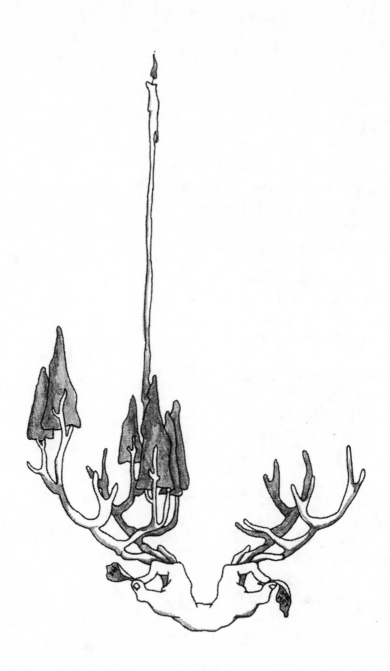

BY WENDY PENG

HAND

The walls of this room discreetly
fold back their ears
to the sound of doors
opening and closing,
hinges creaking in
the night with rust on its feet.

Her body opens
to the light he pours
into her and together
they travel the alleyways
of ancestral weeping,

the light through the treetops
striking softly at their compound
flesh. He puts his hand
in her soul like a kiss,
sending her tumbling
through forests and glades

into that bleached light
of the tundra where
finally she walks
in his foot-steps
alone.

THE POEMS OF RICHARD SWIFT

BY RICHARD SWIFT

BREASTFED CHARLIE II
(OR RAMBO: FIRST BLOOD)

"UH OH, THE MORONS ARE TAKING OVER"

"WHAT'S THAT?"

"I SAID, THE MORONS ARE TAKING OVER
CHHAARRLLIIEEEE"

XRIGHTXRIGHTXXX
"RIGHT RIGHT... SORRY, I'M REALLY
INTO THIS BOOK RIGHT NOW"

THEY SAT THERE FOR A WHILE IN THE SILENCE
ALL AWKWARD N SHIT

BY RICHARD SWIFT

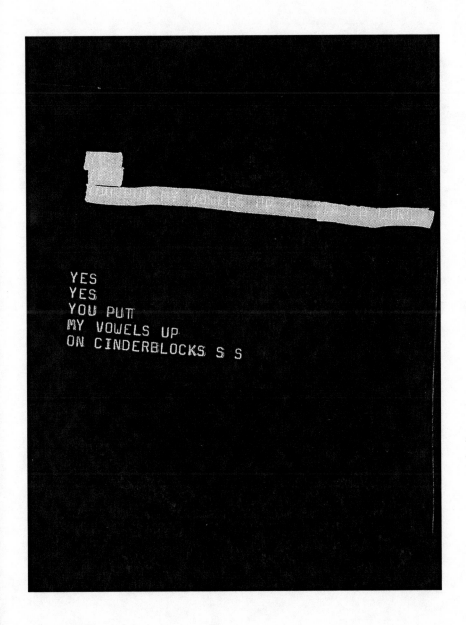

YES
YES
YOU PUT
MY VOWELS UP
ON CINDERBLOCKS S S

BY RICHARD SWIFT

HAPPY VALENTINE'S DAY
I HOPE YOU GOT THE
CARDS I SENT
AND THE FLOWER

LET'S DO ACID TONIGHT

THE POEMS OF RICK LUPERT

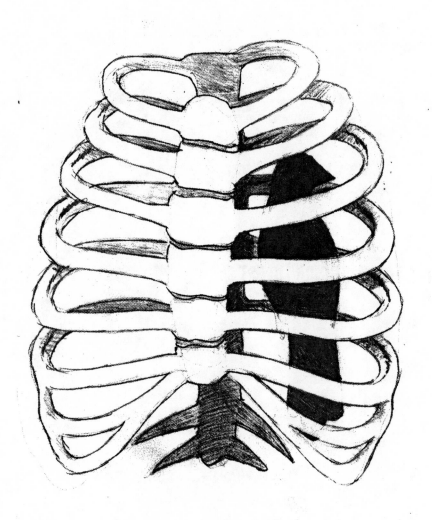

BY BRANDON LYON

ETERNAL EMBRACE FORESEEING

Archaeologists in Italy have discovered a couple buried 5,000 to 6,000 years ago, hugging each other.

ROME (Reuters), Tuesday, February 6, 2007

That's the way I want to go
in her arms, teeth intact

Discovered in five thousand years
a beacon to the loveless masses of the future

Our femurs and tibias co-mingled
a love only bones could know

We'll be like black and white movies
an innocent portrayal of a time long gone

They knew how to do it back then, they'll say
just imagine if they still had eyes

MAKING LOVE TO THE FIFTY FOOT WOMAN

Foreplay takes a week
and you have to buy a ladder

When she says just a little to the left
you have to get there by car

You can have her
in two different neighborhoods at once

Mood music
takes an orchestra

Her bed
a forest

Protection...let's just say
you can get lost in the options

When she finishes
it makes the news

items fall off shelves
bridges collapse

When you finish
she doesn't notice

With a woman so large
Feeling inadequate is normal

She is aware of this
makes you comfortable

looks down at you with her eyes
like two Hubble Telescopes

says to you
with open mouth and legs

Don't worry sweetie;
You're just the right size

BY JENNIFER DAVIS

JEWEL OF SHERMAN OAKS

for Addie

Your hair and legs
your shakes and noises

You may never take out the garbage
but you shouldn't be co-mingling
with the garbage anyway

You lizard lover
shaker maker
bed spooner

occasional cabinet closer
the heat of my apartment
the Jewel of Sherman Oaks

THE POEMS OF ROGER BONAIR-AGARD

FAT-TONGUED
(an ars poetica for Jennifer)

...means my fingers are in your mouth
trying to pull the dirty words we'll need
to take us through this week
this lakeside mountain-town of retirees
and wealthy frat-boys

the words of your bike-trails
and Vermont sugar-house recollections
words that make paths like
syrup cuts along bark

fat-tongued
because black boys aren't always sure
how to negotiate in all this white
how to talk to the woman
in front of me without being Bigger
Thomas and Invisible Man at once
so I feed you poems

in dollop-sized morsels
this is how we talk
go to a place we can both be comfortable
search inside your mouth
for those full-mouthed fat-tongued words
  wheel   circumference   shit
  enlarge   dirt
                fuck

this last in my own accent's most
gritty rounded sound so it'll be a bauble
placed against your palate

where I put it with my own tongue
the only way black boys know
sometimes to come up with a language
even their oppressors might comprehend

BY RICHARD SWIFT

HARVEST

(for A.) (after Carl Phillips)

you do not answer
      and your recorded voice
        reminds me of the gone week
  your throat in my hands
  like a surrendered hart's
your foot a grip of jasmine
in my mouth

so I leave a message
a poem in which a man reveals
the magic of his lover's all night
singing the song of my own voice
mimicking the poet's music

        ...anxious for evening as for
        some beautiful to the bone

        messenger to come. They will open
        again for him. His hands are good.
        His message is a flower.

and I remember three things...

      your short breath caught
      coming under my weight

      your perfect curved feet gripping
      my hips fingers latticed
      around my ribs

      you emerging from the shower
      steam billowing wrapped
      in a single towel
      blooming

THE POEMS OF AMBER TAMBLYN

IN MY BEST ANNE SEXTON ACCENT
For the one who shouldn't have

I dug through your shoulders
and found a love poem
you were going to throw away.
I saved it.

I keep it
with all your love letters
in a parrot's cage that dangles from my ear.

I'm a ballerina tiptoeing across your boredom
in a tutu with no underwear on.

My best Anne Sexton accent sends the caves
searching for their long lost echo
in a sea of yawning mermaids.

Drops by to visit your thoughts unannounced
like the uncle you can never forgive.

Can't keep her eyes off keeping you.

Will wander into the arms of another sense
while grieving for your smell.

Makes the hissing sound of lovers
returning to each other on a holiday.

Doesn't care where your sorrow comes from
as long as it goes somewhere.

Walks the beach at night when the moon is grounded.

Circles the Saturdays in you

hogs all the blankets of your skin

lets you swig on my style
til it creeps up on you like Irish car bombs.

My best Sexton cruises down
your post party boulevard nerves
til something arrests.

Is a homeless, hungry journey
into the shelter of your eyes.

Sleeps clutching your sneakers like a stuffed animal
and dreams of running in a world
that ran away with you.

BY ROBBY MOORING

HE SEEMED LIKE A NICE AXE

You were adept in the Art of slow recoil.
Not a freckle on your face ever cared to surrender.

I stopped counting
the times I couldn't count
on you.

Started the habit of smoking
to forgive your mouth
for giving up mine.

Whose lips did you kiss
that last time we did?

You went for them like a draw.
Like a double-dog dare.

You just gazed at the bridge of my nose
while the dams around it broke.

These eyes like combusting plums,
sadder than a Christmas tree on the 26th.

I should have listened
to all the New England fireflies
who told me not to.

My heart was a wave
that broke for you.

BY ROBBY MOORING

SUNDAY PAPER'S ADVERTISEMENT SECTION
For Pablo

"CLOUD SEEKING CLOUD
FOR RAINBOW GENOCIDE.

MUST BE ABLE TO SPEAK 4 SPECIES OF BIRD
INCLUDING PIGEON, SEAGULL, AND HAWK.

NO STRATO-NIMBUS MOOD SWINGERS PLEASE.
SHAPE SHIFTING AS A HOBBY IS A PLUS.

BUT NO BUTTER MILK GOD COMPLEXES.
SHIFTING INTO SOMEONE'S DEAD CAT TO MAKE THEM CRY
IS NOT ORIGINAL.

I ENJOY CREATING PHALLIC RESTORATIONS,
TORNADO TEASING FARMERS,
AND STEALING SPOTLIGHT FROM ALL THINGS BLUE.

WILLING TO TRADE SKILLS;

AIRPLANE RATTLING
(A GOOD LAUGH WHEN SOMEONE PUKES)

FOR THE ART OF SUNSET MAKING.
(I CAN NEVER GET THOSE RAYS RIGHT.)

MUST BE LONELIER THAN I AM.

ARE YOU WITH ME?

IF SO,
MEET ME ABOVE MOUNT EVEREST TONIGHT.

I'LL BE FLOATING NEXT TO
THE BIG, GLOWING, WHITE MAGNET
ON GOD'S BLACK FRIDGE."

THE POEMS OF SHAPPY SEASHOLTZ

HAIKU

loving you is hard
but not as hard as Dokken
that shit truly rocks

PISS ON MY VALENTINE

To all the elementary school teachers who forced us to
make little mailboxes out of construction paper only
to be filled with pain and rejections...

This one's for you.

To all the snooty girls who giggled at me and made fun
of me and never once gave me one of the those stupid
Kmart valentines...

This one's for you.

To all the people who get balloons and flowers at the
office from their significant others and make a big
to-do about it in front of their lonely single
co-workers...

This one's for you!

To all the people crowding restaurants, throwing fits
in stores and spending over $650 million on this
Hallmark holiday...

This one's for you.

To all the people who asked me if they could bring
their boyfriend or girlfriend to my "Anti-Valentine's
Day" poetry reading...

BY ROBBY MOORING

Yeah, this one's for you!

to all the people who rant and rave about how much
they hate Valentine's day and then weep openly in the
valentine's aisle at Jewel...

This one's for you!

And for all the truly bitter fucks like me who enjoy
wallowing in self-pity...

Hey, this one's for you!

THIS IS A LOVE POEM?

Oooh! She got me!

She got me right where it counts. She awakened my snoozing spirit. She poked me in the third eye with a yummy, creamy, sassafrassy love branch.

I had forgotten my sexual preference before she came around!

I had forgotten how blue my balls could get!

I had forgotten the joy of throwing your money out an open window and saying, "Take it all! I don't care about material things anymore! I'm in love! Do you hear me? I'M IN LOVE!"

I had forgotten how fun it is to hold hands and giggle and skip through dangerous dark city alleyways!

The joy of sucking poisonous venom out of your lover's freshly bit ankle – especially after you told her not to fucking touch your pet snake!

Laughing over the fact that you both had a crush on Loretta Swit in sixth grade!

Arguing about who gets to sleep on the wet spot and getting so frustrated you piss yourself just to get her to be quiet!

The feel of fresh stitches on your bottom lip after she
busted it open for ya!

I had forgotten how awkward awkward silences can be.

How comforting the Bible can be after a drunken
argument about which character we most identify
with in "The Breakfast Club" (Duckie, I insist!).

I had forgotten how "Let's Just Be Friends" feels like
a shot in the nards.

Love be not proud, but it certainly be bullshitty!

THE POEMS OF MICHAEL ROBERTS

FIRE-SWALLOWER

Where is the red storm of your kiss?
The tiger in the burning cage of your mouth?

This is the darkest room in the house.
Even the light bulbs are afraid to come here.
I point them away from the lamps
and they turn from me like sad refugees.

I put the tv in a coma
for telling me lies about love.
I was surprised when it bled from its circuits.

Your red lipstick is still around the cigarette butts.
I wish they were burning.

It is a desperate hour for everything that needs oxygen.
The sky is offering blood for your beauty tonight.
We both crave the saltwater off your bones,
the fire from your fuel.

Twilight has the drunk shivering of swallows,
but my silver heart is coated in gunpowder.

On the littered beach in Mexico
gunpowder from the fireworks
washed away into the ocean
and my heart filled with blue ink.

This is only the threat of a pen.
I couldn't kill anything that breathes.

And everything out this window seems to
Breathe with an anchor in its black lungs.

All the clouds are in the shape of guns
held to the birds' heads.

Until you get home.
Until your spark sets the dark curtains to this world ablaze.

BOX CUTTERS

Lover, smuggle me past airport security
in your purse and we'll give each other
hand jobs in coach under our coats.

Afterwards we'll fall asleep
on strangers' warm shoulders, drool and
dream about fish with glow-in-the-dark organs
swimming under the ice floes thousands of feet beneath us.

Let's remove our safety belts during take-off,
stand up in the aisle and yell, "we'll fight
anyone on this plane for a window seat!"

If the flight attendant gets lippy
mace her and tie her up in the lavatory,
say, "sorry, hon, the snacks were terrible
and the movies suck. They're all American."

We too have terror inside.
Fire lining our stomachs.
Electricity buzzing like fat bees in our veins.

We are pilots for the day.

We may never touch land again.

MUMBLECORE or, CHILE

Low-pitched voices crawl through telephone wires
across miles of storm-traced sky to crackle in your ear,
to speak of love or say goodnight.

Your cell phone lights up a pulse,
someone loves you out there, beyond the drunk
drivers and ambulances, on the other side of the
blacked out apartment buildings and moonlit
skyscrapers.

The words leak out of us, corrupting
the air.

My tongue is a fat red caterpillar
inching along the bottom of my mouth,
swollen with regret.

I say, "I miss you."

You say, "Bless you."

I say, "I didn't sneeze."

This is the scene where we dissolve
to last winter and fall asleep
to the warm hum of tv as we count
the cars going by on the highway like sheep.

You tell me about a dream you had:
You are looking inside my mouth with a flashlight,

your fingerprints are all over the coral walls of my cheeks.
I tell you to stick out your tongue and it rolls out like a map
of South America.
An arrow on the tip indicates YOU ARE HERE.

Tell me more. You are my joy.

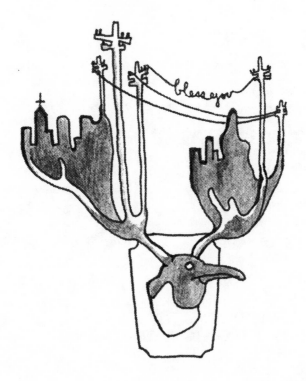

BY WENDY PENG

ASTRONAUTS IN THEIR UNDERWEAR

It's still dark outside.
The sun's a fire in space, but I can't see it from the window.
Darkness spills out of my sockets.
I lay back down next to you.

We are astronauts embracing on the edge of a black hole.
Astronomers of sleep.
We are what I say we are
in this spectral palace, this chaotic bedroom.

I wake you to tell you the time.

"Baby, it's 6:35." I say.
"So."
"Don't you have to be to work at 7?"
"7:30. I already have half of my work clothes on anyway."

She's in her socks and underwear.

She talks to me with her eyes closed.

She gets smaller and smaller
as I rise to the ceiling.

PANTY-NAPPER

At night your panties fly at me from corners of the room
like wild parrots in a tropical storm.
My plan is to trap them and sell them illegally
across the border.

Mexicans will love them and pay top peso.
I know if I was Mexican, I would.
I would rub them in mi amigos' faces
and say, "look at these beautiful panties!"

There are no less than 22 species
in the vivid country of your bedroom.

But they're not all exotic birds. Some are silk fish
swimming to the surface of your sock drawer.
Raccoons break in in the middle of the night
and tease them out of their hiding places.

In the morning I've seen them modeling
your red thongs for the dog.

Your underpants are a pervert's coloring book.

Diego Rivera's fingerprints are all over
your backside.

A thin black veil covers an ass I would confess to
and my heart flashes like a hummingbird's wing
when you walk into the room.

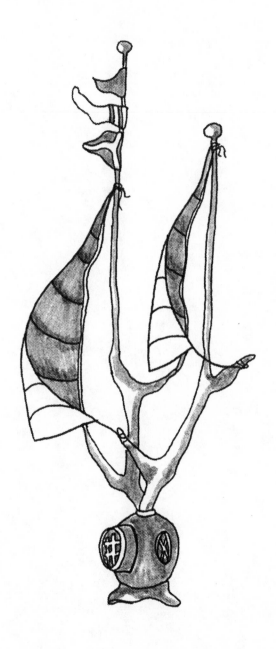

BY WENDY PENG

A POEM BY STEPHEN LATTY

BY BRANDON LYON

TONGUE-LOCK

Love is like a very, very long kiss
that gets disorienting over time;
you lose all context for what it felt like
not to be kissing, kissing all of the time.

Love is like her tongue in your mouth
forever.

People who are not in love, those
who have stuck their tongues somewhere else -- in
the live light-socket of religion, in the community-

slobbered water bowl of politics, in the all-night
buffet of endless 21st Century moneymaking,
onto the frozen flagpole of self and everywhere other
than at the permanent lip-locked play within her mouth.

Love is the breath shared through locked lips.
Nose, that other organ, left to know the world, breathe.

THE POEMS OF MICHAEL C. FORD

THE LAST LOVE POEM

This night I have no charms to make you sleep
Will begin again as your thoughts about me
Crawl out of your brain like woodworms
I am a log in an old forest
You snag my polluted leaves
On untender branches
You hack off my trunk
Drink the brew from my busted bark
I used to think your love was
Soft as flat tires on a
Sparkletts delivery truck
Now it's all tough as a
Trilobitic beginning again
On some cold contaminated
Galapagos Archipelago beach

VALENTINE JUST IN TIME

Her eyes instead of rain
Her skin instead of snow
Her mouth
Instead of sunshine waves
She makes me want to inhale
Olympian lost treasures for lunch, as
Pentagon gods devour the dinners of war
I am walking through these televisions,
Beverly Hills, yellow, hallowed houses of
Her hair
I'm looking through her face
Instead of windows
That's right!
I'm looking through her face
Instead of windows

I LIVE TO SMUGGLE BLUE PLATE SPECIALS OF DEATH INTO THOSE RITZY AND HIGH-ROLLER RESTAURANTS

Truth is a metaphor that
we forgot was a metaphor
-Nietzsche

In the 2nd-grade I fell in love with Kathleen W: never
told her 'til this poem. Never dipped blond braids in
inkwells; only borrowed her eraser, once. Even
though her father was one of the finest mailmen
who ever carried Altadena, I never got a chance to
play post-office. Now, after scored North Central
Valley years corrosive with sophistication: living
like a thief; falling asleep behind the voices of soft
music and hard women. Now, thinking back on one
of those San Joaquin County chicks chalked off the
old existential tote-sheet, y'know, in quite simply
off-the-cuff comparison, y'all understand, 2nd-grade
Kathleen comes up, in my mind
sharp as a steak knife I stole from The Stork Club
in nineteen sixty-four.

BY MATTHEW CARVER

A POEM BY MICHAEL MCCLURE

VALENTINESS
For Amy

THE SPOTTED APPLE'S TASTE?
Is
it
free
or
is
it
structure?
RAPTURE
spreads
in
the
smell
of
APPLE BLOSSOMS
but it is light
on the scale

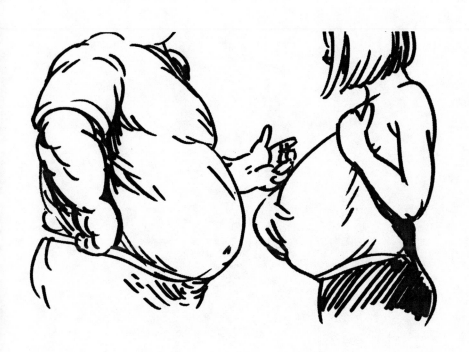

BY MATTHEW CARVER

THE POEMS OF BRENDAN CONSTANTINE

BY BINGHAM

TURKEY AT THE WEASEL DANCE

I am a corsage
They are all smiles

BY BINGHAN

FAT MAN TO HIS BELOVED

Angel,
do you think The Mad Horse
Of History Rides Long Into Fire
would make a good name for a girl?
Yes, My Only Only, I do.
But if we ever have an end
of nights, when the sea scabs over
& every gasp of heaven turns to glass,
we'll name it Little Boy.

BY BINGHAM

LOOK

at the / look at / look at you
you've got the whole / it's like we all /
just look at you / Surprise the curtains /
the car / the lawn and the old / the river
came right to your door. You stepped /
some mornings / and leaf / well you'd
be / swear the whole forest looked into
you / There was a bird / those birds / a
yellow one with / it had a blackness to /
you said it was imitating the electricity
running through / pretty / through / so
clear / a bell with a crystal clapper / as
careful / sounded so / so / you / ! / You

THE POEMS OF DERRICK BROWN

BY MATTHEW CARVER

THE UNLIMITED NOISES OF SCIENCE.

There is this older woman.
She falls upon me like an avalanche of slave diamonds.

She has a problem with her eye. Maybe cataracts.
I have a problem with my ears. Artillery.
I bang into her.

Mountain goats, locking horns--- over and over on the cliff
and no one wins.

She got the noises of science.
Train noises bellow from her joints.
She is always departing.

There they go, those canary fingernails, chipped in nicotene
pulling at my hips until she docks
her fat French tongue.

Some words drift in her mouth like dead birds in the shore break.

She rolls her pantyhose down until they look like doughnuts
revealing legs like shipyard pliers.
She gives the necessary kiss.
It is snarly.

I say, "You kiss me like I'm the last."
She replies, "You might be."

My chambers hiss.
Her teeth get lost inside me like surgical weapons.
I spit out the window.
Now the night feels loose.

"Fix me. Fix me with all your fingers."
I think she's winking at me.
The lights in here look like they could go out at any minute.
We got a radio with a broken antennae. I wonder what she hears?
It plays all night and we both miss somebody else.

THE RIDGE

The sun dropped warm silhouette cloaks around us
at the third act of twilight.

"Look at you." she said.

We stood upon the margins of horizon at the ridge of a Spring Hill
Battle ground.

She was staring at my ankles.

She said, "Except for the bottoms of your feet, you're in the air.
You are always in the air... and the sky does not stop...until here.
The sky starts at our feet."

It was so dumb, it was true. Her arms lifting like toy bridges around her
form.
She went to the ground slowly.
Colors spreading out from her dress
like a box of crayons left on a July sidewalk.

I tried to hold her, horny as anything prehistoric.
I told her she had a bug exploring for a place to bite her kneecap
and she acted like it should be there.

I wanted to make that pure mind tremble...
Her innocence was frightening.
No seduction. No strategy in stillness.

She was teaching me how to just be.

BY MATTHEW CARVER

I laid my arm across her and it sank like a cathedral in Venice.
A day, as boring as a color-coded community closed up shop.
She had me. I had her.

A rose in the teeth
of a sleepy matador.

BY MATTHEW CARVER

POETRY COMES AFTER THE FACT

Look at you,
dressed up like a short story.

Easy on the eyes and punchy.

Another night beach trespass
and I laid on the rocks with you like all teen movie finales.
You kissed like a runway virgin
and strolled like a whore outta money.

You spoke soft as a wet mint and soothed me like a new air conditioner.

Like all bartenders on slow days, you listened.
You wished I had called you more
like all far away Mothers do.

"I don't learn anything from your poetry."

I say, "I do."

She scooted her pants down the long beach towel in the blue tide light.
"I'm worried about the sand," She said, naked and dangling.
I wanted to convince her I was a writer.

"Wow. It looks like a box of newly opened surgical gloves."
I've said some untimely things in my life.

"Write a poem about it, weirdo."

Poetry for me is looking back.
I don't know what now is."

"Shut up and get to work."

Except for 'Yes'
words don't really matter when there is a lust
as pure as new drugs
as fine
as your first sober screw.

YOU ARE THE OPERA

Some singers write songs
and struggle in a spinning Laundromat combat
wadding up the night
hunting for something to sing about.

Your holy ghost is a song that's been clawing it's way out for years.

It's a loud one-
brighter than nightmare lightning.

You are not just the light,
you're the end of the tunnel.

You are the opera.

No one can rewrite you.

BY MATTHEW CARVER

ACKNOWLEDGEMENTS

All of these authors are amazing. Their bio's are massive.
To contact artists, email writebloody@gmail.com or google their name
and city. All poems copyrights by each author. Reprinted with permis-
sion of author and publisher. No poem may be used without expressed
consent by the author.

JEFFREY MCDANIEL *(Published by Manic D Press)*	Philadelphia / NYC
MINDY NETTIFEE	Long Beach CA
JACK HIRSCHMAN	San Francisco CA
BUCKY SINISTER	San Francisco CA
CRISTIN O'KEEFE APTOWICZ	NYC / Philadelphia
ANIS MOJGANI	Portland / New Orleans
MICHAEL CIRELLI	NYC
JOHN GARDINER	Laguna Beach CA
BEAU SIA	Los Angeles CA
BUDDY WAKEFIELD	Seattle WA
LYNNE PROCOPE	NYC
NATHAN WILLET	Long Beach CA
VICTOR INFANTE	Worcester MA
AGNETA FALK	San Francisco CA
RICHARD SWIFT	Oregon
RICK LUPERT	Sherman Oaks CA
ROGER BONAIR-AGARD	NYC
AMBER TAMBLYN	Venice Beach CA
SHAPPY SEASHOLTZ	Chicago / NYC
MICHAEL ROBERTS	Orange County CA
STEPHEN LATTY	Venice Beach CA
MICHAEL C. FORD	Los Angeles CA
MICHAEL MCCLURE	San Francisco CA
BRENDAN CONSTANTINE	Hollywood CA
DERRICK BROWN	Nashville TN

OTHER WRITE BLOODY BOOKS

WHAT IT IS, WHAT IT IS
Graphic Art Prose Concept book by Maust and author Paul Maziar

LIVE FOR A LIVING
New Poetry compilation by Buddy Wakefield

SOME THEY CAN'T CONTAIN
Poetry compilation by Buddy Wakefield

SCANDALABRA
New poetry compilation by Derrick Brown (Summer 2008)

I LOVE YOU IS BACK
Poetry compilation (2004-2006) by Derrick Brown

BORN IN THE YEAR OF THE BUTTERFLY KNIFE
Poetry anthology, 1994-2004 by Derrick Brown

LETTING MYSELF GO
Prose by Buzzy Enniss

COCK FIGHTERS, BULL RIDERS, AND OTHER SONS OF BITCHES
Photographic Odyssey by M. Wignall (Winter 2008)

Printed in the United States
101062LV00002B/271-345/A